Party Wall etc. A

An
Easy Guide
(second edition)

A M Frame Msc MRICS FFPWS FASI FCIOB MCMI
Chartered Building Surveyor and Chartered Building Consultant

Published by
THE FACULTY OF PARTY WALL SURVEYORS
P O Box 86
Rye
TN31 9BN

Telephone: 01424 883300
Email: enq@fpws.org.uk
Website: www.fpws.org.uk

First Edition 2014
Second Edition 2017

First Published in England
by
The Faculty of Party Wall Surveyors

All rights reserved
Copyright 2014 by A M Frame

Acknowledgments:
Illustrations: Malcolm Lelliott
Legal: Stuart J Frame

Please note: Throughout this book genders are taken as both male and female as are the singular
and plural interpretations.

FOREWORD

In 1997 the Government introduced party wall legislation across the whole of England and Wales in the form of the Party Wall etc. Act 1996. Unfortunately there was little in the way of guidance for the general public and surveyors alike to undertake the work associated with this Act.

The Faculty of Party Wall Surveyors sought to help in this matter and set about providing education by way of teaching seminars and guide books for both the general public and surveyors.

The Faculty of Party Wall Surveyors (FPWS) now has a strong membership of trained surveyors and runs a telephone advice line for all those that need assistance in dealing with party wall work.

This Easy Guide has been prepared to help you understand some of the key elements of the Act and we trust that it will answer many of your questions.

The Faculty of Party Wall Surveyors
P O Box 86
Rye
TN31 9BN

Telephone: 01424 883300
Email: enq@fpws.org.uk
Website: www.fpws.org.uk

CONTENTS

Introduction   Page   5
                The Act
                The Purpose of the Act

Part I   Definitions   7
                Party Wall
                Party Fence Wall
                Building Owner
                Adjoining Owner
                Party Wall Surveyor
                Line of Junction
                Notices
                Schedule of Condition
                Award

Part II   The Main Parts of the Act   19
                Section 1   The Line of Junction
                Section 2   Works to the Party Wall
                Section 6   Excavation Work
                Section 7   Compensation
                Section 8   Rights of Access
                Section 10   Resolving the Dispute

Part III   The Party Wall Surveyor   32
                The Appointment of Surveyors
                The Third Surveyor

Part IV   The Award   35

Part V   The Works   37

Part VI   Frequently Asked Questions   38

Part VII   Example Letters and Notices   42

Part VIII   Party Wall etc. Act 1996   48

Part IX   Further Information   79
                Flow Chart

INTRODUCTION

Party Wall etc. Act 1996 ('the Act')

The Act came into force on the 1st July 1997 and applies throughout England and Wales. It does not apply to Scotland or Northern Ireland.

The Act does not remove the need for Town Planning, Building Regulation or any other statutory requirements.

This explanatory booklet is given as a guide and it is not the Act itself nor does it supersede it. It merely seeks to provide clarification and assistance to those wishing to undertake building works on a boundary or to party walls and structures, whilst simultaneously assisting those who are affected by such works. The guide does not cover every aspect of the Act and any further advice should be sought from The Faculty of Party Wall Surveyors.

The Purpose of the Act

The purpose of the Act is to put a framework in place in which issues over certain building works can be resolved without expensive legal action between neighbours. The Act is designed to assist owners in conducting their proposed work whilst at the same time providing protection to the adjoining owners (neighbours) insofar as they may be affected.

The Act is therefore designed to enable various works to proceed without hindrance and not to place obstacles in the way of the progress of the works. If the adjoining owner dissents to a notice served on him this does not mean that he can stop the works proceeding. Instead it means that he has the right to appoint a party wall surveyor to prepare and serve an award that would take into consideration the adjoining owner's rights as well as authorising the time and manner of execution of the proposed works.

Basically the Act sets out precisely what can be done when building works are proposed that may have an effect upon the adjoining property.

The Act is applicable in the following simplified situations:

1. Building on a 'line of junction' (i.e. boundary) that is not already built upon.
2. Undertaking various works to an existing party wall or a boundary wall.
3. Excavating within certain distances of the adjoining property.

PART I
Definitions

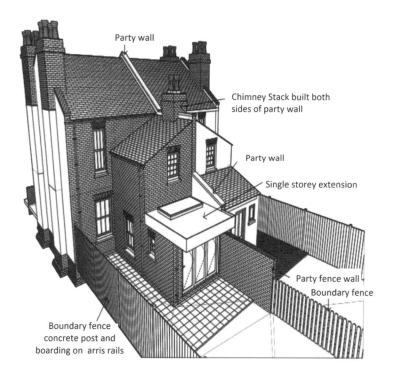

PERSPECTIVE OF REAR EXTENSION

Party wall type "B" where single storey encloses upon adjoining property including roof. Remainder of exposed wall (hatched) is not a party wall.

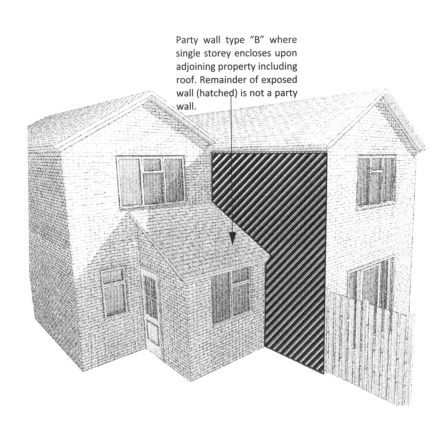

Party Wall
As defined in section 20 of the Act, this is a wall which either
a) forms part of a building and stands on lands belonging to different owners

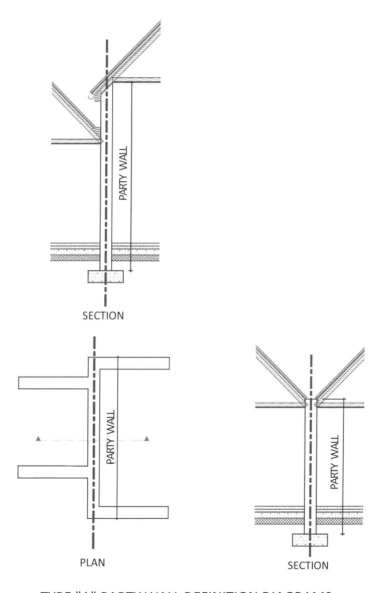

SECTION

PLAN

SECTION

TYPE "A" PARTY WALL DEFINITION DIAGRAMS

or
b) so much of a wall as separates buildings belonging to different owners

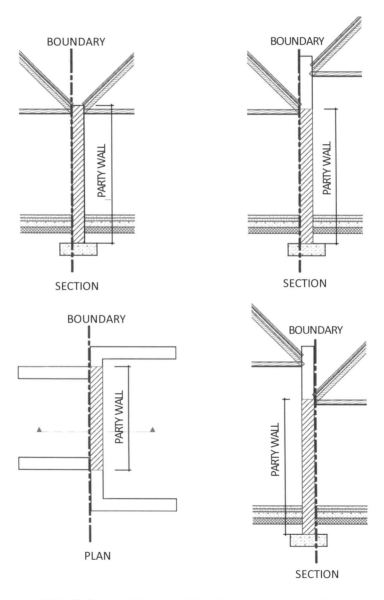

TYPE "B" PARTY WALL DEFINITION DIAGRAMS

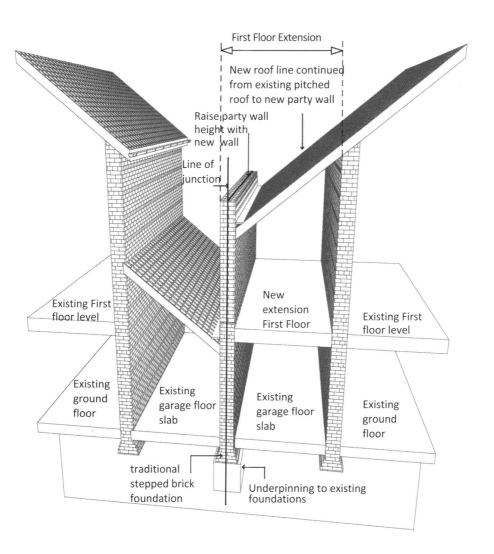

First Floor Extension

New roof line continued from existing pitched roof to new party wall

Raise party wall height with new wall

Line of junction

Existing First floor level

New extension First Floor

Existing First floor level

Existing ground floor

Existing garage floor slab

Existing garage floor slab

Existing ground floor

traditional stepped brick foundation

Underpinning to existing foundations

SECTION THROUGH PARTY WALL

11

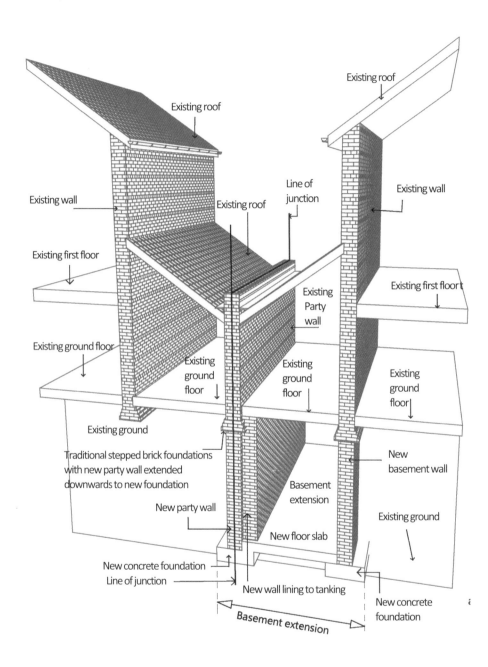

Existing roof

Existing roof

Existing roof

Line of junction

Existing wall

Existing wall

Existing wall

Existing roof

Existing first floor

Existing Party wall

Existing first floor

Existing ground floor

Existing ground floor

Existing ground floor

Existing ground floor

Existing ground

Traditional stepped brick foundations with new party wall extended downwards to new foundation

New basement wall

New party wall

Basement extension

Existing ground

New floor slab

New concrete foundation
Line of junction

New wall lining to tanking

New concrete foundation

Basement extension

PARTY WALL WITH BASEMENT EXTENSION

Party Fence Wall

This is a wall which does not form part of a building and stands on lands belonging to different owners, such as a garden wall, but it does not include a timber fence.

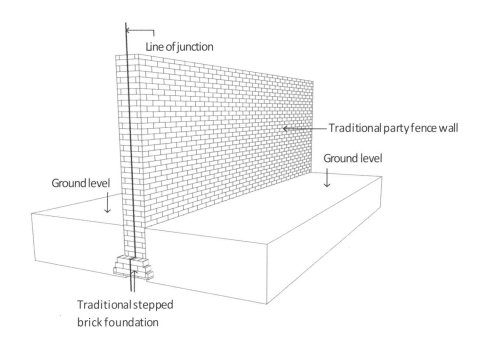

Line of junction

Traditional party fence wall

Ground level

Ground level

Traditional stepped
brick foundation

PARTY FENCE WALL

Dividing boundary wall on lands
of two different ownerships.

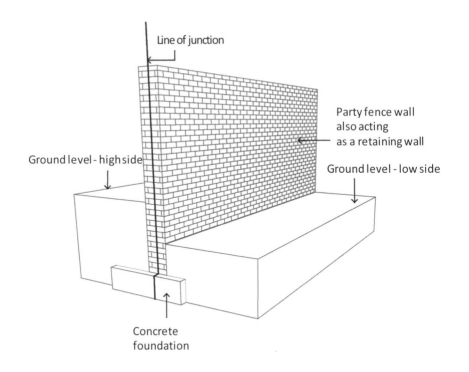

Line of junction

Party fence wall also acting as a retaining wall

Ground level - high side

Ground level - low side

Concrete foundation

PARTY FENCE WALL

Wall acting as retaining wall.

Party Structure

This is a party wall and also a floor partition or other structure separating buildings or parts of buildings. Typically this is a floor/ceiling in a block of flats.

Building Owner

This is a person or company that is proposing to undertake the building works and who is either the freeholder or has a lease for longer than one year.

Adjoining Owner
This is a person or company who is either the freeholder or has a lease for longer than one year of the property adjoining that of the building owner.

Adjoining Occupier
This is a person or company who is the occupier of the adjoining property, but who does not qualify as an adjoining owner.

Surveyor
This is a person who is appointed by the building owner or adjoining owner to resolve any dispute between the building owner and adjoining owner which is connected with any work to which the Act relates.

Any person may potentially act as a party wall surveyor except the respective owners, who are not allowed to act for themselves. It is however usual to appoint professional people such as surveyors, architects, engineers etc. who are experienced in the workings of the Act. The Faculty of Party Wall Surveyors, who specifically deal with party wall matters, can provide you with names of party wall surveyors in your area.

Each party may appoint their own chosen surveyor or each party may appoint a single surveyor. In the latter case the surveyor is known as the 'agreed surveyor'. It is envisaged that an 'agreed surveyor' would be used in smaller, less complicated residential works for example.

Line of Junction
This is, for the purposes of this guide, another name for a boundary. It is the meeting point of lands that are in different ownership.

Notices
A notice is a written communication by the building owner informing the adjoining owner of the works he proposes to undertake. There are some suggested sample notices in Part VII of this booklet that may be used together with suggested sample replies. A notice may even be in

the form of a simple letter but for any notice to be valid it needs to comply with the specific provisions in the Act. This will vary according to what type of works are proposed and therefore under what section of the Act the notice is served. In summary however, notices should contain information about the works that are proposed, and when the owner would like to commence those works.

It should be carefully noted that the Act is not invoked by a building owner unless he serves the relevant notice on the adjoining owner (although the Act may be used by agreement between the parties where no notice has been served).

Section 1 of the Act concerns works involving new walls built up to, or astride the line of junction, and a notice period of one month is required before the works can commence.

Section 2 of the Act concerns works to an existing party wall or structure, and a notice period of two months is required before the works can commence.

Section 6 of the Act concerns excavating (such as digging for foundations, drains or reducing the level of the ground) to certain depths and within certain distances of the adjoining owner's building or structure and a notice period of one month is required before works can commence.

The Act says that it is the duty of the building owner to serve the relevant notice on the adjoining owner. However, very often this is done by a surveyor acting on the building owner's behalf, providing that the surveyor has been given written authority by the building owner to do so.

Once a notice is served the adjoining owner has the choice to either expressly consent in writing to the proposed works as set out in the notice, or to dispute them. If no reply is forthcoming within fourteen days, an adjoining owner is generally deemed to have disputed the works in the notice.

However, it must be noted that the building owner and adjoining owner may come to any agreement about the works at any stage. In such a case they will not need to rely on any award made by the surveyors.

It is important to remember that consenting to a notice does not mean that an adjoining owner has no protection under the Act. All the protection and rights that the Act provides to an adjoining owner remain available if necessary, even where a notice is consented to.

If a notice is disputed, then the parties must appoint a surveyor to act for them. The surveyor(s) will draw up an 'award' which sets out the building owner's right to conduct his proposed works, and the time and manner of execution of those works.

Schedule of Condition

A schedule of condition is a written record of the condition of the adjoining owner's property before the work starts. It should record any existing defects or damage to avoid any future dispute over whether the building owner's works have caused any damage. It usually describes the walls, floors and ceilings, or indeed any other parts that may be affected by the works, such as the garden fence or planting. Photographs usually support the schedule of condition.

Preparing a schedule of condition is not a specific requirement of the Act, but it is most prudent and common practice to do so, and all competent party wall surveyors would be likely to advise that this be done.

If an adjoining owner does not wish to grant access in order to prepare a schedule of condition then it is possible that an award may be made without one. However, in the event that damage occurs it may be more difficult for the adjoining owner to prove that the damage is attributable to the building owner's works. It is therefore highly advisable that such a record is made.

An increasingly common scenario is for adjoining owners to consent to a notice served on them, but on the condition that a schedule of condition is taken of their property first.

Award
An award is a legal document prepared by the surveyor(s). There is no specific format that an award should take, but common standard clauses often appear. It basically has five parts.

1. The sections of the Act that apply with the names and addresses of all the parties and surveyors concerned.
2. The description of the works permitted to be undertaken.
3. The rights and requirements of the two owners and the appointed surveyors in relation to the works.
4. Particular clauses dealing with the execution of the works including any expenses and compensation etc. that may be payable, and the liability for the surveyors' costs.
5. The signature(s) of the surveyor(s) and date.

An award should confine itself to the work as specified in the notices and generally not include matters unrelated to those works. For example, if the notice is served under section 6 of the Act, which only relates to excavation work, then such matters as the building that is erected upon the foundations are irrelevant as they do not fall within the Act's remit.

The award should not include matters relating to any easements, covenants, planning conditions, personal matters between the parties, or generally anything unrelated to the intended works.

PART II
The Main Parts of the Act

Section 1 – The Line of Junction – land that is not built on from either side.

If a building owner intends to build a wall 'on' (i.e. 'astride') the line of junction he must serve a notice of his intention to do so upon the adjoining owner. In such circumstances the notice must be served at least one month before the works are due to commence.

A building owner may propose to build up to or astride the line of junction.

Upon receipt of the notice the adjoining owner may consent to the works, and should give this consent in writing to the building owner.

If the adjoining owner does not consent and a dispute arises between the owners, then party wall surveyors will need to be appointed to resolve the dispute.

Please note that it is a misunderstanding that there is a right to place projecting foundations on an adjoining owner's land under this section. There is only a right to do so if such projecting foundations are proven to be 'necessary', which is not usually the case given modern construction methods.

Section 2 – Works to the party wall, party fence wall, party structure, or boundary wall.

This would entail such works as;

(a) Making the existing party wall higher e.g. forming a mansard roof for a loft conversion.
(b) Underpinning a party wall.
(c) Making structural repairs to a party wall.
(d) To build a new party wall to comply with the latest building regulations.
(e) Installing steel beams into a party wall.
(f) To demolish and rebuild a party wall.
(g) Removing a chimney from a party wall.
(h) To cut away any projections from a boundary wall in order to build a new wall against it.
(i) To cut into a boundary wall to insert a flashing.
(j) To expose a party wall to the weather that was previously enclosed.

The above list is just some of the more common works that arise, but many other works are also covered by this section.

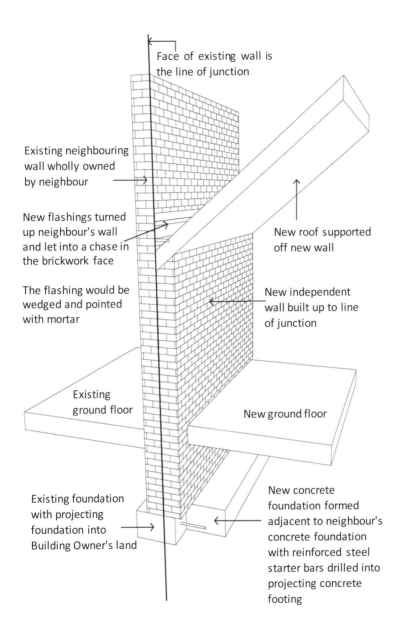

Face of existing wall is the line of junction

Existing neighbouring wall wholly owned by neighbour

New flashings turned up neighbour's wall and let into a chase in the brickwork face

The flashing would be wedged and pointed with mortar

New roof supported off new wall

New independent wall built up to line of junction

Existing ground floor

New ground floor

Existing foundation with projecting foundation into Building Owner's land

New concrete foundation formed adjacent to neighbour's concrete foundation with reinforced steel starter bars drilled into projecting concrete footing

NEW WALL BUILT UP TO LINE OF JUNCTION
& NEIGHBOURING STRUCTURE

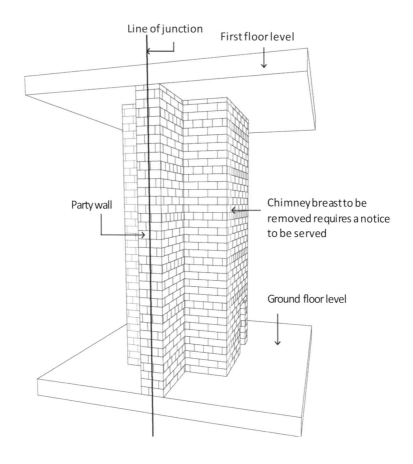

Line of junction

First floor level

Party wall

Chimney breast to be removed requires a notice to be served

Ground floor level

CHIMNEY STACK ON PARTY WALL

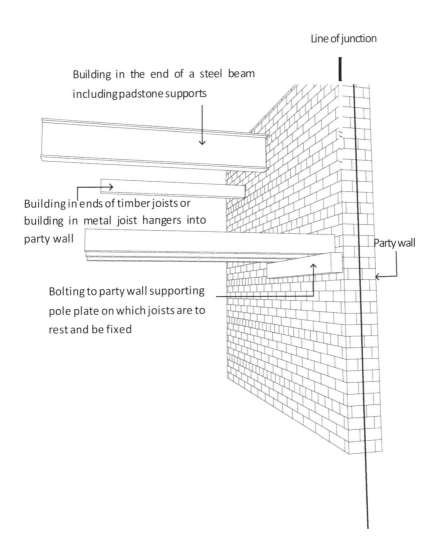

Line of junction

Building in the end of a steel beam including padstone supports

Building in ends of timber joists or building in metal joist hangers into party wall

Party wall

Bolting to party wall supporting pole plate on which joists are to rest and be fixed

BUILDING INTO OR ON A PARTY WALL WITH STRUCTURES

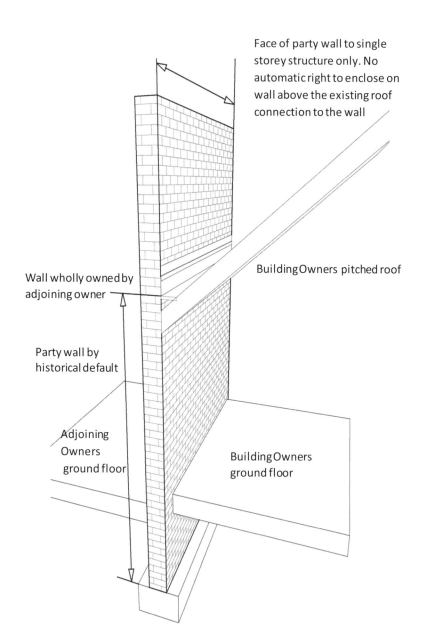

Face of party wall to single storey structure only. No automatic right to enclose on wall above the existing roof connection to the wall

Building Owners pitched roof

Wall wholly owned by adjoining owner

Party wall by historical default

Adjoining Owners ground floor

Building Owners ground floor

WALL WHOLLY OWNED BY ADJOINING OWNER

24

If a building owner intends to undertake any such works he must serve a notice of his intention to do so upon the adjoining owner. In such circumstances the notice must be served at least two months before the works are due to commence.

Upon receipt of the notice the adjoining owner may consent to the works and should give this consent in writing to the building owner within 14 days.

If the adjoining owner does not provide such consent within 14 days by a notice in writing then a dispute is deemed to arise between the owners and a party wall surveyor or surveyors will need to be appointed to resolve the dispute.

Section 6 – Excavation Work within certain distances from the adjoining property.

If a building owner wishes to excavate, (for example for foundations, drains or to build a basement) within a three metre distance of an adjoining building or structure and the excavation will be to a lower depth than the lowest part of adjoining owner's foundation then he must serve a notice of his intention to do so upon the adjoining owner, which in this section means any owner of a building or structure within three metres and not just the immediate neighbour.

In such circumstances the notice must be served at least one month before the works are due to commence.

If a building owner wishes to excavate within six metres of the adjoining owner's building or structure, and deeper than the adjoining owner's building or structure, so that the excavations fall within a 45^0 plane drawn downwards from the lowest level of the adjoining owner's foundations then he must also serve a notice.

Again, the adjoining owner here means any owner of a building or structure within six metres, not just the immediate neighbour.

The position of the boundary is therefore not relevant under this section.

As this part is more complex you are advised to seek the advice and help of a party wall surveyor.

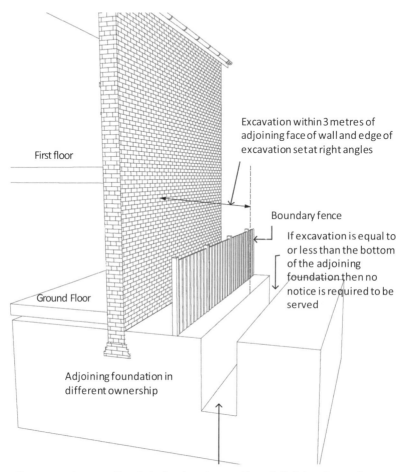

Excavation within 3 metres of adjoining face of wall and edge of excavation set at right angles

First floor

Boundary fence

If excavation is equal to or less than the bottom of the adjoining foundation then no notice is required to be served

Ground Floor

Adjoining foundation in different ownership

If proposed excavation is to be dug deeper than Adjoining Owner's foundation bottom then this is notifiable if within 3 metres. If deeper and more than 3 metres away from Adjoining Owner's foundation then the 6 metre distance rule will apply.

EXCAVATION WITHIN 3 METRES OF AN ADJOINING BASEMENT IN DIFFERENT OWNERSHIP

27

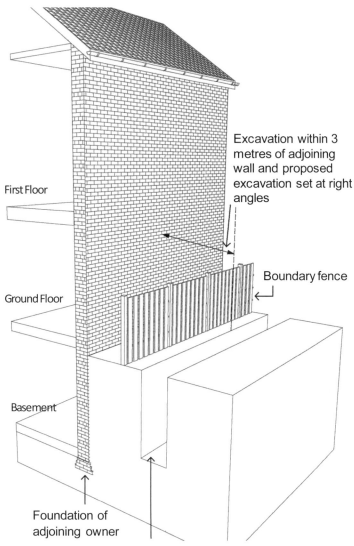

First Floor

Excavation within 3
metres of adjoining
wall and proposed
excavation set at right
angles

Boundary fence

Ground Floor

Basement

Foundation of
adjoining owner

Proposed excavation, although deep, do not go below foundations
adjacent to the basement and therefore are not notifiable. Be aware
that the basement may not be present long the whole length of the
proposed excavation and there could be a requirement to notify.

EXCAVATION WITHIN 3 METRES OF ADJOINING
FOUNDATION IN DIFFERENT OWNERSHIP

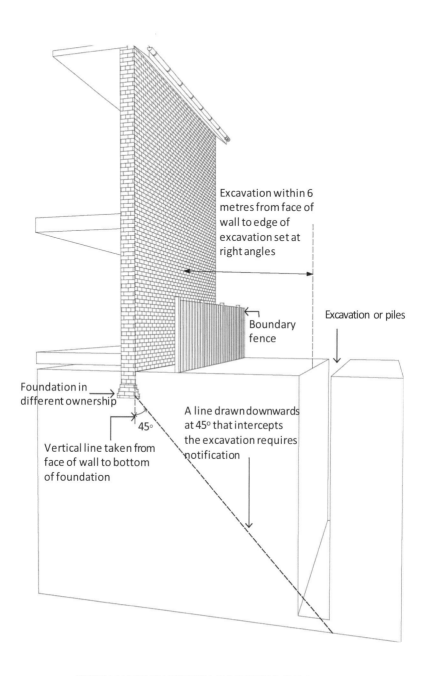

Excavation within 6 metres from face of wall to edge of excavation set at right angles

Boundary fence

Excavation or piles

Foundation in different ownership

45°

Vertical line taken from face of wall to bottom of foundation

A line drawn downwards at 45° that intercepts the excavation requires notification

EXCAVATION WITHIN 6 METRES OF A
FOUNDATION IN DIFFERENT OWNERSHIP

Upon receipt of the notice the adjoining owner may consent to the works and should give this consent in writing to the building owner within 14 days.

If the adjoining owner does not consent then a dispute is deemed to arise between the owners and a party wall surveyor or surveyors will need to be appointed to resolve the dispute.

Section 7 – Compensation

Building work is quite often noisy and messy and generally some inconvenience must be expected when such work is undertaken. However, unnecessary inconvenience should not be expected and the works should be carefully planned to avoid such.

The Act does allow for compensation to be paid by the building owner to the adjoining owner for any loss or damage caused by the works, and that compensation is usually determined by the appointed surveyors. Compensation for any loss or damage can also be awarded to an adjoining occupier, as well as the adjoining owner.

Section 8 – Rights of Access

The Act gives certain rights to the building owner and his workers to enter the premises of the adjoining owner during working hours, upon giving 14 days written notice. However such access must be restricted to the purpose of undertaking the specified works in the Act.

There is therefore no right to enter the adjoining owner's land for other works outside of the Act's remit – only works in pursuance of the Act attract a right of access. The surveyors are also entitled to access over the adjoining owner's land in order to fulfil the purpose for which they are appointed.

Careful advice needs to be taken when dealing with this particular section.

Section 10 – Resolving the Dispute

This is a major part of the Act and relates to the appointment of a party wall surveyor or surveyors.

It deals with the situation where a dispute has arisen between the building owner and the adjoining owner, and the appointment of surveyor(s) is therefore made in order to resolve that dispute.

It is important to understand the role of the party wall surveyor and how he resolves the dispute between the owners in accordance with the Act. This is explained in more detail in Part III.

PART III
The Party Wall Surveyor

The Appointment of Surveyors

It is emphasised that an adjoining owner can consent to a notice served on him. In such circumstances surveyors do not need to be appointed by the parties and an award regulating the works does not need to be made. Consenting to a notice does not mean that an adjoining owner loses the rights available to him under the Act (such as the right for compensation for damage caused by the works).

However, where a notice has not been consented to, then surveyors need to be appointed to produce an award which regulates the proposed works. It is very important to choose your surveyor wisely, because once the surveyor is appointed the Act does not allow an owner to rescind the appointment and appoint someone else.

The surveyor's appointment is a statutory appointment, and must be made in writing. The surveyor's duty is to settle the dispute between the parties in accordance with the Act. He is not 'employed' as such by either the building owner or the adjoining owner and nor does he generally act as their 'agent'. His appointment is personal to him and not to the company or firm that he might work for.

The surveyor should not act as an adversarial advocate but should administer his duties under the Act as impartially as possible. The surveyor nevertheless does have a duty to listen to and consider his appointing owner's concerns, and ensure that he has all the necessary information required to settle the dispute between the parties fairly and in accordance with the Act. However, it should be noted that a party wall surveyor does not act as the agent for the party appointing him, and retains a high level of independence from his appointing owner.

The parties may appoint their own surveyor to act for them, or they can agree to appoint a single surveyor, and of course this should save in costs. In this case both parties must provide a written appointment requesting the surveyor to act as an 'agreed surveyor'. An agreed surveyor should ideally be used in relation to relatively minor or uncomplicated works, which are usually found in residential settings.

The appointment of an agreed surveyor should be carefully considered and ideally he should not be the designer of the project, as there may be a perceived conflict of interest, albeit it is probably lawful for a designer to do so.

An important point to remember in appointing an agreed surveyor is that there will be no 'third surveyor' in place. This means that if either of the owners becomes unhappy with the agreed surveyor, they will have no one to refer matters to in order to assist them, unlike the situation where two surveyors are appointed, one by each owner, in which situation a third surveyor would also be in place (see following for details about the third surveyor).

One of the surveyor's duties will be to check that all the 'paperwork' is correct, which means he will need to confirm that:

1. The names and addresses of all the owners of the properties (building owners and adjoining owners);
2. The notice(s) served is (are) valid;
3. The surveyor's appointment has been made in writing.
4. The name and address of the selected third surveyor (if required in the case where two surveyors are appointed) is agreed.

The surveyor(s) should not act if the above requirements have not been fulfilled.

One of the actions taken before the commencement of the works will be to record the schedule of condition of the adjoining owner's property. This is not part of the Act and is therefore not a legal requirement, however it is most prudent to do so, as such a record may avoid any future disagreement in the event that damage is alleged to have occurred.

It must be remembered that party wall surveyors are appointed to resolve disputes between the owners and this is why an award is made by the surveyor(s). Resolving the statutory dispute that has arisen between the parties is the party wall surveyor's primary duty.

The Third Surveyor
If each party appoints a surveyor then those two surveyors must select another surveyor called the 'third surveyor'. This is the very first of their duties and MUST be done. This third surveyor is in place to act as a referee to resolve disputes between the two surveyors, or to generally assist in matters. It is important to note that he may also be contacted by either of the two owners on any matter relating to the dispute, and over the heads of the party appointed surveyors if necessary. The parties have an absolute right to approach the third surveyor to assist matters. This may occur if the two party appointed surveyors are not acting effectively and/or cannot agree on matters.

Each owner should therefore be informed of their right to contact the third surveyor from the outset, and they should request the name and address of the selected 'third surveyor' in the event that either of them wishes to contact him directly.

The surveyors (or the third surveyor as the case may be) resolve the dispute between the parties by making an award – see part IV.

Part IV
The Award

As previously mentioned an award is a legally binding document prepared by a party wall surveyor, or surveyors, for the benefit of both the building owner and the adjoining owner. It is prepared to resolve a dispute that has arisen between the two owners.

The award provides statutory authorisation to the building owner to conduct his works, and usually in a specific manner and during specific times. An award often contains a number of other ancillary matters relating to the proposed works. Where a dispute has arisen between the owners, it is only until the award is made and served that the building owner is entitled to start work.

Whilst the award is prepared by the surveyor(s) their role is to act impartially throughout. This means that apart from the gathering of information they are not acting on instructions from either the building owner or the adjoining owner in preparing the award.

It is important that the detail an award contains is factually correct.

Once the award is prepared it is served upon both the building owner and the adjoining owner. Service of the award should, as a matter of good practice, be done simultaneously.

Should either owner be unhappy with the award they may appeal the award in the county court. This must be done within 14 days of being served with the award. If the award is not appealed, then it becomes legally binding and cannot subsequently be challenged, even via the courts.

If it is felt that the award is incorrect or unfair an advisable first step might be to speak with the appointed surveyor and he will explain the actions taken in more detail. This approach may then deal with any queries and thus avoid the cost of having to appeal the award in the court.

Under the Act, if either of the owners or either of the surveyors appointed ask the third surveyor to determine the disputed matter(s) then the third surveyor will be entitled to make the necessary award.

Part V
The Works

After the award has been served (or the initiating notice has been consented to) the building owner may carry out the works authorised by the award (or as set out in the notice if the notice has been consented to). The works should be in strict compliance with the requirements set out in the award.

The building owner is not obliged to undertake the awarded works, the award merely permits him to conduct such works if he so desires, but if he does he must comply with the conditions laid down in the award.

It may be that notices have to be given with regards to gaining access to the adjoining owner's property for example.

It should be noted that it is not the role of the party wall surveyors to supervise or 'police' the works; they are neither project managers or contract administrators. However, the surveyors should be notified if any breaches of the award occur or if damage to the adjoining owner's property occurs.

Should any problems arise relating to the works stipulated in the award, then the appointed surveyors should be contacted to resolve the matter.

There is no official 'sign off' but at the end of the works the party wall surveyors often re-inspect the adjoining owner's property to ensure that all is in order, which usually means checking the schedule of condition to note if any damage has been caused by the works.

Part VI
Frequently Asked Questions

These are some of the common questions asked but you may have many more questions and the FPWS will answer these if you contact them direct. Contact details are given in Part IX.

Q1.   What happens if I do not serve a notice as required under the Act?

A1.   The Act carries no fines or penalties but it is possible that the adjoining owner may apply to the court for an injunction ordering you to stop work.

Q2.   What happens if the adjoining owner does not consent to the notice within 14 days?

A2.   Under section 1 of the Act, where you wish to build a new wall on the line of junction, you will have the right to only build on your own land.

In respect of a notice served relating to works under sections 2 and 6 of the Act, if there is no reply to the notice after 14 days then a dispute is deemed to have arisen, and you and the adjoining owner must appoint a surveyor. If the adjoining owner then still fails to respond and appoint a surveyor, then after giving him ten days to do so, you may appoint a surveyor on his behalf.

Q3.   What happens if I do not agree with what my appointed surveyor is doing?

A3.   You are unable to rescind his appointment, but you can approach the third surveyor to resolve the matter for you. However if you have chosen to have just the one 'agreed surveyor', then there is no third surveyor that can be called upon.

This is why you should take care in appointing a surveyor and more particularly when appointing the one 'agreed surveyor'.

Q4.   Do I have to inform my neighbour if I am just putting up bookshelves or fixing electrical socket outlets to the party wall?

A4.   This sort of work would generally be considered to be so minor that such works would not need to be notified under the Act. However, much will also depend on the individual circumstances in each case.

Q5.   What do the surveyors do?

A5.   The surveyors prepare the award, which is a legal document between the two owners. The surveyors normally meet at the property and prepare a schedule of condition (although not a requirement of the Act) which assists all parties, as any damage that may be caused can be checked against it, and compensation awarded if required.

Q6.   Who pays the surveyors' fees?

A6.   Under normal circumstances the building owner would pay the fees, (known as 'costs') as he is the one undertaking the works, usually for his benefit. However, the surveyors will make the final determination, and can make the adjoining owner pay their costs, for example in circumstances where he has been particularly obstructive.

Q7.   What if I do not agree with the contents of the award?

A7.   Both the building owner and the adjoining owner can appeal the award in the county court within 14 days of being served the award. You should probably, of course, speak with your appointed surveyor on the matter before doing so, as he may be able to answer your queries.

Q8.　　As a building owner, do I / my builders have the right of access to my neighbour's property to undertake the work, and as an adjoining owner do I have to grant access to the building owner to undertake the work?

A8.　　There is generally a right of access, within working hours to undertake the notifiable works but 14 days written notice must be provided to the adjoining owner.

Q9.　　I have doubts as to whether the building owner can complete the work properly.

A9.　　If you are in doubt on this, you can by notice require the building owner to set aside an amount of money, as agreed between yourselves or determined by the surveyors, as security that would allow the works that affect you to be completed.

Q10.　　Does the Act override other legal rights?

A10.　　Common law rights are supplanted by the Act where, for example, the works would be liable to attract actions in trespass or nuisance. The Act therefore takes precedence on any matter for which it makes provision. Other rights, such as existing easements or covenants, for example, are not however affected.

Q11.　　Can the Act be used to resolve a boundary dispute?

A11.　　No. The Act is not there to resolve such matters and the surveyors do not have any power to do so.
Practically speaking, in the event that the boundary is not agreed the Act cannot be applied until the matter is resolved. This would not apply in the case of a Section 6 notice, which only deals with an excavation within a certain distance of the adjoining owner's building or structure and where the position of the boundary is irrelevant.

However, the surveyors can, for the purposes of deciding whether they have jurisdiction under the Act, make a decision as to where the line of junction (boundary) lies, but it should be noted that this will not have the same status as a legally determined boundary, such as by a court or Land Registry.

Part VII
Example Letters and Notices

Example letter for use with all notices (Italics need to completed/amended as necessary)

*Name and Address
of Building Owner*

Name and Address of Adjoining Owner

Date...........................

Dear ....

Re: Party Wall etc. Act 1996 – *Address of building works*

I *(we)* write to advise you that I *(we) Name and address of Building Owner* serve upon you the enclosed notice setting out the proposed works that are likely to affect the premises, known as *address of adjoining premises.*

This letter is to explain, in less formal terms, that there are three options open to you, and are itemised for clarity as follows:

1. You may consent to the works, in which case please sign the enclosed form with the appropriate section completed and return to it me *(us)*. Although not a requirement under the Act, I *(we)* would advise that a schedule of condition be prepared prior to the commencement of the works that will be checked upon completion to ensure that no damage has occurred.

2. If you do not consent to the works, or if there is a matter in dispute arising from them that cannot be readily resolved between us, you therefore must appoint a surveyor in

accordance with the Act. This surveyor may be a single agreed surveyor nominated by us both who will act impartially to decide the matters in issue, in which case please return the enclosed form with the appropriate section completed.

3. As an alternative to the appointment of an agreed surveyor, you may in accordance with the Act, appoint a second surveyor of your own choice to act solely for you, in which case please return the enclosed form with the appropriate section completed.

I *(we)* enclose a copy of the explanatory booklet to help you understand the process.

Yours sincerely

Name of Building Owner

Party Wall etc. Act 1996
Line of Junction Notice
Sections 1(2) and 1(5)

Italics need to completed/amended as necessary

To   *Name and Address of Adjoining Owner*

I *(we)*   *Name and Address of Building Owner*

As Owner(s) of the land and premises known as

     Address of Building Site

Which adjoins your premises known as

     Address of Adjoining Owner's premises

Hereby serve notice on you under Section *1(2) / 1(5)* [delete as applicable] and the proposed works, which are:

     Describe the wall that is proposed to be built

I *(we)* propose to start the works after the expiration of one month from the date of this Notice or earlier if you agree.

Signed................................ *Building Owner*   Date....................

Party Wall etc. Act 1996
Party Structure Notice
Section 2

Italics need to completed/amended as necessary

To   *Name and Address of Adjoining Owner*

I *(we)* *Name and Address of Building Owner*

As Owner(s) of the land and premises known as

Address of Building Site

Which adjoins your premises known as

Address of Adjoining Owner's premises

Hereby serve NOTICE on you under Section 2 and the accompanying drawings show the proposed works, which are:

Describe the works, and if possible, relate them to the specific paragraphs of section 2(2).

I *(we)* propose to start the works after the expiration of two months from the date of this Notice or earlier if you agree.

Signed................................. *Building Owner*   Date..........................

Party Wall etc. Act 1996
Three Metre/Six Metre Notice
Section 6

Italics need to completed/amended as necessary

To   *Name and Address of Adjoining Owner*

I *(we)*   *Name and Address of Building Owner*

As Owner(s) of the land and premises known as

Address of Building Site

Which adjoins your premises known as

Address of Adjoining Owner's premises

Hereby serve NOTICE on you under Section 6(5) and the accompanying drawings show the proposed works including the depth of the excavation and its site, which are:

Describe the works and attach the drawings.

Insert a paragraph about whether or not you are underpinning safeguarding etc. as per section 6(6).

I *(we)* propose to start the works after the expiration of one month from the date of this Notice or earlier if you agree.

Signed…......................…*Building Owner*   Date….......................

Party Wall etc. Act 1996
Acknowledgement of Notice
All sections

Italics need to completed/amended as necessary

I *(we) Name and Address of Adjoining Owner*

Having received the Notice served by

Name and Address of Building Owner

In respect of the land and premises known as

Address of Building Site

Concerning works under *Section 1 Line of Junction*
Section 2 Party Structure
Section 6 Three Metre/Six Metre

Consent to the Works/Dissent from the Works – *Delete as appropriate*
(In the event of consent no surveyor will be appointed)

And agree to the appointment of the Agreed Surveyor

Name and Address of Agreed Party Wall Surveyor

And would appoint

Name and Address of Party Wall Surveyor

As my *(our)* Party Wall Surveyor

Signed...........................*Name of Adjoining Owner*   Date.................

Part VIII
Party Wall etc. Act 1996

1996 Chapter 40

ARRANGEMENT OF SECTIONS

Construction and repair of walls on line of junction

Section
1. New building on line of junction.
2. Repair etc. of party wall: rights of owner.
3. Party structure notices.
4. Counter notices.
5. Disputes arising under sections 3 and 4.

Adjacent excavation and construction
6. Adjacent excavation and construction.

Rights etc.
7. Compensation etc.
8. Rights of entry.
9. Easements.

Resolution of disputes
10. Resolution of disputes.

Expenses
11. Expenses.
12. Security for expenses.
13. Account for work carried out.
14. Settlement of account.

Miscellaneous
15. Service of notices etc.
16. Offences.

17. Recovery of sums.
18. Exception in case of Temples etc.
19. The Crown.
20. Interpretation.
21. Other statutory provisions.

General
22. Short title, commencement and extent.

Party Wall etc. Act 1996

1996 CHAPTER 40

An Act to make provision in respect of party walls, and excavation and construction in proximity to certain buildings or structures; and for connected purposes. [18th July 1996]

BE IT ENACTED by the Queen's most Excellent Majesty, by and with the advice and consent of the Lords Spiritual and Temporal, and Commons, in this present Parliament assembled, and by the authority of the same, as follows:-

Construction and repair of walls on line of junction

New building on line of junction.
1.-(1) This section shall have effect where lands of different owners adjoin and-

(a) are not built on at the line of junction; or
(b) are built on at the line of junction only to the extent of a boundary wall (not being a party fence wall or the external wall of a building),

and either owner is about to build on any part of the line of junction.

(2) If a building owner desires to build a party wall or party fence wall on the line of junction he shall, at least one month before he intends the building work to start, serve on any adjoining owner a notice which indicates his desire to build and describes the intended wall.

(3) If, having been served with notice described in subsection (2), an adjoining owner serves on the building owner a notice indicating his consent to the building of a party wall or party fence wall-

(a) the wall shall be built half on the land of each of the two owners or in such other position as may be agreed between the two owners; and

(b) the expense of building the wall shall be from time to time defrayed by the two owners in such proportion as has regard to the use made or to be made of the wall by each of them and to the cost of labour and materials prevailing at the time when that use is made by each owner respectively.

(4) If, having been served with notice described in subsection (2), an adjoining owner does not consent under this subsection to the building of a party wall or party fence wall, the building owner may only build the wall-

(a) at his own expense; and

(b) as an external wall or a fence wall, as the case may be, placed wholly on his own land,

and consent under this subsection is consent by a notice served within the period of 14 days beginning with the day on which the notice described in subsection (2) is served.

(5) If the building owner desires to build on the line of junction a wall placed wholly on his own land he shall, at least one month before he intends the building work to start, serve on any adjoining owner a notice which indicates his desire to build and describes the intended wall.

(6) Where the building Owner builds a wall wholly on his own land in accordance with subsection (4) or (5) he shall have the right, at any time in the period which-

(a) begins one month after the day on which the notice mentioned in the subsection concerned was served, and

(b) ends twelve months after that day,

to place below the level of the land of the adjoining owner such projecting footings and foundations as are necessary for the construction of the wall.

(7) Where the building owner builds a wall wholly on his own land in accordance with subsection (4) or (5) he shall do so at his own expense and shall compensate any adjoining owner and any adjoining occupier for any damage to his property occasioned by-

(a) the building of the wall;
(b) the placing of any footings or foundations placed in accordance with subsection (6).

(8) Where any dispute arises under this section between the building owner and any adjoining owner or occupier it is to be determined in accordance with section 10.

Repair etc. of party wall: rights of owner.
2.-(1) This section applies where lands of different owners adjoin and at the line of junction the said lands are built on or a boundary wall, being a party fence wall or the external wall of a building, has been erected.

(2) A building owner shall have the following rights-

(a) to underpin, thicken or raise a party structure, a party fence wall, or an external wall which belongs to the building owner and is built against a party structure or party fence wall;

(b) to make good, repair, or demolish and rebuild, a party structure or party fence wall in a case where such work is

52

necessary on account of defect or want of repair of the structure or wall;

(c) to demolish a partition which separates building belonging to different owners but does not conform with statutory requirements and to build instead a party wall which does so conform;

(d) in the case of buildings connected by arches or structures over public ways or over passages belonging to other persons, to demolish the whole or part of such buildings, arches or structures which do not conform with statutory requirements and to rebuild them so that they do so conform;

(e) to demolish a party structure which is of insufficient strength or height for the purposes of any intended building of the building owner and to rebuild it of sufficient strength or height for the said purposes (including rebuilding to a lesser height or thickness where the rebuilt structure is of sufficient strength and height for the purpose of any adjoining owner);

(f) to cut into a party structure for any purpose (which may be or include the purpose of inserting a damp course);

(g) to cut away from a party wall, party fence wall, external wall or boundary wall any footing or any projecting chimney breast, jamb or flue, or other projection on or over the land of the building owner in order to erect, raise or underpin any such wall or for any other purpose;

(h) to cut away or demolish parts of any wall or building of an adjoining owner overhanging the land of the building owner or overhanging a party wall, to the extent that it is necessary to cut away or demolish the parts to enable a vertical wall to be erected or raised against the wall or building of the adjoining owner;

(j) to cut into the wall of an adjoining owner's building in order to insert a flashing or other weather-proofing of a wall erected against that wall;

(k) to execute any other necessary works incidental to the connection of a party structure with the premises adjoining it;

(l) to raise a party fence wall, or to raise such a wall for use as a party wall, and to demolish a party fence wall and rebuild it as a party fence wall or as a party wall;

(m) subject to the provisions of section 11(7), to reduce, or to demolish and rebuild, a party wall or party fence wall to –

(i) a height of not less than two metres where the wall is not used by an adjoining owner to any greater extent than a boundary wall; or

(ii) a height currently enclosed upon by the building of an adjoining owner;

(n) to expose a party wall or party structure hitherto enclosed subject to providing adequate weathering.

(3) Where work mentioned in paragraph (a) of subsection (2) is not necessary on account of defect or want of repair of the structure or wall concerned, the right falling within that paragraph is exercisable-

(a) subject to making good all damage occasioned by the work to the adjoining premises or to their internal furnishings and decorations; and

(b) where the work is to a party structure or external wall, subject to carrying any relevant flues and chimney stacks up to such a height and in such materials as may be agreed between the building owner and the adjoining owner concerned or, in the event of dispute, determined in accordance with section 10;

and relevant flues and chimney stacks are those which belong to an adjoining owner and either form part of or rest on or against the party structure or external wall.

(4) The right falling within subsection (2)(e) is exercisable subject to-

(a) making good all damage occasioned by the work to the adjoining premises or to their internal furnishings and decorations; and

(b) carrying any relevant flues and chimney stacks up to such a height and in such materials as may be agreed between the building owner and the adjoining owner concerned or, in the event of dispute, determined in accordance with section 10;

and relevant flues and chimney stacks are those which belong to an adjoining owner and either form part of or rest on or against the party structure.

(5) Any right falling within subsection (2)(f),(g) or (h) is exercisable subject to making good all damage occasioned by the work to the adjoining premises or to their internal furnishings and decorations.

(6) The right falling within subsection (2)(j) is exercisable subject to making good all damage occasioned by the work to the wall of the adjoining owner's building.

(7) The right falling within subsection (2)(m) is exercisable subject to-

(a) reconstructing any parapet or replacing an existing parapet with another one; or

(b) constructing a parapet where one is needed but did not exist before.

(8) For the purposes of this section a building or structure which was erected before the day on which this Act was passed shall be deemed to conform with statutory requirements if it conforms with the statutes regulating buildings or structures on the date on which it was erected.

Party structure notices.
3.- (1) Before exercising any right conferred on him by section 2 a building owner shall serve on any adjoining owner a notice (in this Act referred to as a "party structure notice") stating-

(a) the name and address of the building owner;

(b) the nature and particulars of the proposed work including, in cases where the building owner proposes to construct special foundations, plans, sections and details of construction of the special foundations together with reasonable particulars of the loads to be carried thereby; and

(c) the date on which the proposed work will begin.

(2) A party structure notice shall-

(a) be served at least two months before the date on which the proposed work will begin;

(b) cease to have effect if the work to which it relates-

(i) has not begun within the period of twelve months beginning with the day on which the notice is served; and

(ii) is not prosecuted with due diligence.

(3) Nothing in this section shall-

(a) prevent a building owner from exercising with the consent in writing of the adjoining owners and of adjoining occupiers any right conferred on him by section 2; or

(b) require a building owner to serve any party structure notice before complying with any notice served under any statutory provisions relating to dangerous or neglected structures.

Counter notices.
4.-(1) An adjoining owner may having been served with a party structure notice serve on the building owner a notice (in this Act referred to as a "counter notice") setting out-

(a) in respect of a party fence wall or party structure, a requirement that the building owner build in or on the wall or structure to which the notice relates such chimney copings, breasts, jambs or flues, or such piers or recesses or other like works, as may reasonably be required for the convenience of the adjoining owner;

(b) in respect of special foundations to which the adjoining owner consents under section 7(4) below, a requirement that the special foundations-

(i) be placed at a specified greater depth than that proposed by the building owner; or

(ii) be constructed of sufficient strength to bear the load to be carried by columns of any intended

building of the adjoining owner, or both.

(2) A counter notice shall-

(a) specify the works required by the notice to be executed and shall be accompanied by plans, sections and particulars of such works; and

(b) be served within the period of one month beginning with the day on which the party structure notice is served.

(3) A building owner on whom a counter notice has been served shall comply with the requirements of the counter notice unless the execution of the works required by the counter notice would-

(a) be injurious to him;

(b) cause unnecessary inconvenience to him; or

(c) cause unnecessary delay in the execution of the works pursuant to the party structure notice.

Disputes arising under sections 3 and 4.
5. - If an owner on whom a party structure notice or a counter notice has been served does not serve a notice indicating his consent to it within the period of fourteen days beginning with the day on which the party structure notice or counter notice was served, he shall be deemed to have dissented from the counter notice and a dispute shall be deemed to have arisen between the parties.

Adjacent excavation and construction.
6.- (1) This section applies where-

(a) a building owner proposes to excavate, or excavate for

and erect a building or structure, within a distance of three metres measured horizontally from any part of a building or structure of an adjoining owner; and

(b) any part of the proposed excavation, building or structure will within those three metres extend to a lower level than the level of the bottom of the foundations of the building or structure of the adjoining owner.

(2) This section also applies where-

(a) a building owner proposes to excavate, or excavate for and erect a building or structure, within a distance of six metres measured horizontally from any part of a building or structure of an adjoining owner; and

(b) any part of the proposed excavation, building or structure will within those six metres meet a plane drawn downwards in the direction of the excavation, building or structure of the building owner at an angle of forty-five degrees to the horizontal from the line formed by the intersection of the plane of the level of the bottom of the foundations of the building or structure of the adjoining owner with the plane of the external face of the external wall of the building or structure of the adjoining owner.

(3) The building owner may, and if required by the adjoining owner shall, at his own expense underpin or otherwise strengthen or safeguard the foundations of the building or structure of the adjoining owner so far as may be necessary.

(4) Where the buildings or structures of different owners are within the respective distances mentioned in subsection (1) and (2) the owners of those buildings or structures shall be deemed to be adjoining owners for the purposes of this section.

(5) In any case where this section applies the building owner shall, at least one month before beginning to excavate, or excavate for and erect a building or structure, serve on the adjoining owner a notice indicating his proposal and stating whether he proposes to underpin or otherwise strengthen or safeguard the foundations of the building or structure of the adjoining owner.

(6) The notice referred to in subsection (5) shall be accompanied by plans and sections showing-

    (a) the site and depth of any excavation the building owner proposes to make;

    (b) if he proposes to erect a building or structure, its site.

(7) If an owner on whom a notice referred to in subsection (5) has been served does not serve a notice indicating his consent to it within the period of fourteen days beginning with the day on which the notice referred to in subsection (5) was served, he shall be deemed to have dissented from the notice and a dispute shall be deemed to have arisen between the parties.

(8) The notice referred to in subsection (5) shall cease to have effect if the work to which the notice relates-

    (a) has not begun within the period of twelve months beginning with the day on which the notice was served; and

    (b) is not prosecuted with due diligence.

(9) On completion of any work executed in pursuance of this section the building owner shall if so requested by the adjoining owner supply him with particulars including plans and sections of the work.

(10) Nothing in this section shall relieve the building owner from any liability to which he would otherwise be subject for injury to any adjoining owner or any adjoining occupier by reason of work executed by him.

Rights etc. Compensation etc.
7.- (1) A building owner shall not exercise any right conferred on him by this Act in such a manner or at such time as to cause unnecessary inconvenience to any adjoining owner or to any adjoining occupier.

(2) The building owner shall compensate any adjoining owner and any adjoining occupier for any loss or damage which may result to any of them by reason of any work executed in pursuance of this Act.

(3) Where a building owner in exercising any right conferred on him by this Act lays open any part of the adjoining land or building he shall at his own expense make and maintain so long as may be necessary a proper hoarding, shoring or fans or temporary construction for the protection of the adjoining land or building and the security of any adjoining occupier.

(4) Nothing in this Act shall authorise the building owner to place special foundations on land of an adjoining owner without his previous consent in writing.

(5) Any works executed in pursuance of this Act shall-

(a) comply with the provisions of statutory requirements; and

(b) be executed in accordance with such plans, sections and particulars as may be agreed between the owners or in the event of dispute determined in accordance with section10;

and no deviation shall be made from those plans, sections and particulars except such as may be agreed between the owners (or surveyors acting on their behalf) or in the event of dispute determined in accordance with section 10.

Rights of entry

8.- (1) A building owner, his servants, agents and workmen may during working hours enter and remain on any land or premises for the purpose of executing any work in pursuance of this Act and may remove any furniture or fittings or take any other action necessary for that purpose.

(2) If the premises are closed, the building owner, his agent and workmen may, if accompanied by a constable or other police officer, break open any fences or doors in order to enter the premises.

(3) No land or premises may be entered by any person under subsection (1) unless the building owner serves on the owner and the occupier of the land or premises-

(a) in case of emergency, such notice of the intention to enter as may be reasonably practicable;

(b) in any other case, such notice of the intention to enter as complies with subsection (4).

(4) Notice complies with this subsection if it is served in a period of not less than fourteen days ending with the day of the proposed entry.

(5) A surveyor appointed or selected under section 10 may during usual working hours enter and remain on any land or premises for the purpose of carrying out the object for which he is appointed or selected.

(6) No land or premises may be entered by a surveyor under subsection (5) unless the building owner who is a party to the dispute concerned serves on the owner and the occupier of the land or premises-

(a) in case of emergency, such notice of the intention to enter as be reasonably practicable;

(b) in any other case, such notice of the intention to enter as complies with subsection (4).

Easements.
9.- Nothing in this Act shall-

(a) authorise any interference with an easement of light or other easements in or relating to a party wall; or

(b) prejudicially affect any right of any person to preserve or restore any right or other thing in or connected with a party wall in case of the party wall being pulled down or rebuilt.

Resolution of disputes
10.- (1) Where a dispute arises or is deemed to have arisen between a building owner and an adjoining owner in respect of any matter connected with any work to which this Act relates either-

(a) both parties shall concur in the appointment of one surveyor (in this section referred to as an "agreed surveyor"); or

(b) each party shall appoint a surveyor and the two surveyors so appointed shall forthwith select a third surveyor (all of whom are in this section referred to as "the three surveyors").

(2) All appointments and selections made under this section shall be in writing and shall not be rescinded by either party.

(3) If an agreed surveyor-

(a) refuses to act;

(b) neglects to act for a period of ten days beginning with the day on which either party serves a request on him;

(c) dies before the dispute is settled; or

(d) becomes or deems himself incapable of acting,

the proceedings for settling such dispute shall begin *de novo.*

(4) If either party to the dispute-

(a) refuses to appoint a surveyor under subsection (1)(b), or

(b) neglects to appoint a surveyor under subsection (1)(b) for a period of ten days beginning with the day on which the other party serves a request on him,

the other party may make the appointment on his behalf.

(5) If, before the dispute is settled, a surveyor appointed under paragraph (b) of subsection (1) by a party to the dispute dies, or becomes or deems himself incapable of acting, the other party who appointed him may appoint another surveyor in his place with the same power and authority.

(6) If a surveyor-

(a) appointed under paragraph (b) of subsection (1) by a party to the dispute; or

(b) appointed under subsection (4) or (5),

refuses to act effectively, the surveyor of the other party may proceed to act *ex parte* and anything so done by him shall be as effectual as if he had been an agreed surveyor.

(7) If a surveyor-

(a) appointed under paragraph (b) of subsection (1) by a party to the dispute; or

(b) appointed under subsection (4) or (5),

neglects to act effectively for a period of ten days beginning with the day on which either party or the surveyor of the other party serves a request on him, the surveyor of the other party may proceed to act *ex parte* in respect of the subject matter of the request and anything so done by him shall be as effectual as if he had been an agreed surveyor.

(8) If either surveyor appointed under subsection (1)(b) by a party to the dispute refuses to select a third surveyor under subsection (1) or (9), or neglects to do so for a period of ten days beginning with the day on which the other surveyor serves a request on him-

(a) the appointing officer; or

(b) in cases where the relevant appointing officer or his employer is a party to the dispute, the Secretary of State,

may on the application of either surveyor select a third surveyor who shall have the same power and authority as if he had been selected under subsection (1) or subsection (9).

(9) If a third surveyor selected under subsection (1)(b)-

(a) refuses to act;

(b) neglects to act for a period of ten days beginning with

the day on which either party or the surveyor appointed by either party serves a request on him; or

(c) dies, or becomes or deems himself incapable of acting, before the dispute is settled,

the other two of the three surveyors shall forthwith select another surveyor in his place with the same power and authority.

(10) The agreed surveyor or as the case may be the three surveyors or any two of them shall settle by award any matter-

(a) which is connected with any work to which this Act relates, and

(b) which is in dispute between the building owner and the adjoining owner.

(11) Either of the parties or either of the surveyors appointed by the parties may call upon the third surveyor selected in pursuance of this section to determine the disputed matters and he shall make the necessary award.

(12) An award may determine-
(a) the right to execute any work;

(b) the time and manner of executing any work; and

(c) any other matter arising out of or incidental to the dispute including the costs of making the award;

But any period appointed by the award for executing any work shall not unless otherwise agreed between the building owner and the adjoining owner begin to run until after the expiration of the period prescribed by this Act for service of the notice in respect of which the dispute arises or is deemed to have arisen.

(13) The reasonable costs incurred in-

(a) making or obtaining an award under this section;

(b) reasonable inspections of work to which the award relates; and

(c) any other matter arising out of the dispute,

shall be paid by such of the parties as the surveyor or surveyors making the award determine.

(14) Where the surveyors appointed by the parties make an award the surveyors shall serve it forthwith on the parties.

(15) Where an award is made by the third surveyor-

(a) he shall, after payment of the costs of the award, serve it forthwith on the parties or their appointed surveyors; and

(b) if it is served on their appointed surveyors, they shall serve it forthwith on the parties.

(16) The award shall be conclusive and shall not except as provided by this section be questioned in any court.

(17) Either of the parties to the dispute may, within the period of fourteen days beginning with the day on which an award made under this section is served on him, appeal to the county court against the award and the county court may-

(a) rescind the award or modify it in such manner as the court thinks fit: and

(b) make such order as to costs as the court thinks fit.

Expenses

11.- (1) Except as provided under this section expenses of work under this Act shall be defrayed by the building owner.

(2) Any dispute as to responsibility for expenses shall be settled as provided in section 10.

(3) An expense mentioned in section 1(3)(b) shall be defrayed as there mentioned.

(4) Where work is carried out in exercise of the right mentioned in section 2(2)(a), and the work is necessary on account of defect or want of repair of the structure or wall concerned, the expenses shall be defrayed by the building owner and the adjoining owner in such proportion as has regard –

    (a) the use which the owners respectively make or may make of the structure or wall concerned; and

    (b) responsibility for the defect or want of repair concerned, if more than one owner makes use of the structure or wall concerned.

(5) Where work is carried out in exercise of the right mentioned in section 2(2)(b) the expenses shall be defrayed by the building owner and the adjoining owner in such proportion as has regard to –

    (a) the use which the owners respectively make or may make of the structure or wall concerned; and

    (b) responsibility for the defect or want of repair concerned, if more than one owner makes use of the structure or wall concerned.

(6) Where the adjoining premises are laid open in exercise of the right mentioned in section 2(2)(e) a fair allowance in respect of disturbance and inconvenience shall be paid by the building owner to the adjoining owner or occupier.

(7) Where a building owner proposes to reduce the height of a party wall or party fence wall under section 2(2)(m) the adjoining owner may serve a counter notice under section 4 requiring the building owner to maintain the existing height of the wall, and in such case the adjoining owner shall pay to the building owner a due proportion of the cost of the wall so far as it exceeds-

(a) two metres in height; or

(b) the height currently enclosed upon by the building of the adjoining owner.

(8) Where the building owner is required to make good damage under this Act the adjoining owner has a right to require that the expenses of such making good be determined in accordance with section 10 and paid to him in lieu of the carrying out of work to make the damage good.

(9) Where –
    (a) works are carried out, and
    (b) some of the works are carried out at the request of the adjoining owner or in pursuance of a requirement made   by him,

he shall defray the expenses of carrying out the works requested or required by him.

(10) Where –

(a) consent in writing has been given to the construction of special foundations on land of an adjoining owner; and

(b) the adjoining owner erects any building or structure and its cost is found to be increased by reason of the existence of the said foundations,

the owner of the building to which the said foundations belong shall, on receiving an account with any necessary invoices and other supporting documents within the period of two months beginning with the day of the completion of the work by the adjoining owner, repay to the adjoining owner so much of the cost as is due to the existence of the said foundations.

(11) Where use is subsequently made by the adjoining owner of work carried out solely at the expense of the building owner the adjoining owner shall pay a due proportion of the expenses incurred by the building owner in carrying out that work; and for this purpose he shall be taken to have incurred expenses calculated by reference to what the cost of the work would be if it were carried out at the time when that subsequent use is made.

Security for expenses
12.- (1) An adjoining owner may serve a notice requiring the building owner before he begins any work in the exercise of the rights conferred by this Act to give such security as may be agreed between the owners or in the event of dispute determined in accordance with section 10.

(2) Where –

(a) in the exercise of the rights conferred by this Act an adjoining owner requires the building owner to carry out any work the expenses of which are to be defrayed in whole or in part by the adjoining owner; or

(b) an adjoining owner serves a notice on the building owner under subsection (1).

The building owner may before beginning the work to which the requirement or notice relates serve a notice on the adjoining owner requiring him to give such security as may be agreed between the owners or in the event of dispute determined in accordance with section 10.

(3) If within the period of one month beginning with –

(a) the day on which a notice is served under subsection (2); or

(b) in the event of dispute, the date of the determination by the surveyor or surveyors,

the adjoining owner does not comply with the notice or the determination, the requirement or notice by him to which the building owner's notice under that subsection relates shall cease to have effect.

Account for work carried out.
13.- (1) Within the period of two months beginning with the day of the completion of any work executed by a building owner of which the expenses are to be wholly or partially defrayed by an adjoining owner in accordance with section 11 the building owner shall serve on the adjoining owner an account in writing showing-

(a) particulars and expenses of the work; and

(b) any deductions to which the adjoining owner or any other person is entitled in respect of old materials or otherwise;

and in preparing the account the work shall be estimated and valued at fair average rates and prices according to the nature of the work, the locality and the cost of labour and materials prevailing at the time when the work is executed.

(2) Within the period of one month beginning with the day of service of the said account the adjoining owner may serve on the building owner a notice stating any objection he may have thereto and thereupon a dispute shall be deemed to have arisen between the parties.

(3) If within that period of one month the adjoining owner does not serve notice under subsection (2) he shall be deemed to have no objection to the account.

Settlement of account.
14.- (1) All expenses to be defrayed by an adjoining owner in accordance with an account served under section 13 shall be paid by the adjoining owner.

(2) Until an adjoining owner pays to the building owner such expenses as aforesaid the property in any works executed under this Act to which the expenses relate shall be vested solely in the building owner.

Miscellaneous.
15.- (1) A notice or other document required or authorised to be served under this Act may be served on a person;

(a) by delivering it to him in person;

(b) by sending it by post to him at his usual or last-known residence or place of business in the United Kingdom; or

(c) in the case of a body corporate, by delivering it to the secretary or clerk of the body corporate at its registered or principal office or sending it by post to the secretary or clerk of that body corporate at that office.

(1A) A notice or other document required or authorised to be served under this Act may also be served on a person ("the recipient") by means of an electronic communication, but only if—

(a) the recipient has stated a willingness to receive the notice or document by means of an electronic communication,

(b) the statement has not been withdrawn, and

(c)the notice or document was transmitted to an electronic address specified by the recipient.

(1B) A statement under subsection (1A) may be withdrawn by giving a notice to the person to whom the statement was made.

(1C) For the purposes of subsection (1A)—

"electronic address" includes any number or address used for the purposes of receiving electronic communications;

"electronic communication" means an electronic communication within the meaning of the Electronic Communications Act 2000; and

"specified" means specified in a statement made for the purposes of subsection (1A).".

(2) In the case of a notice or other document required or authorised to be served under this Act on a person as owner of premises, it may alternatively be served by –

(a) addressing it "the owner" of the premises (naming them), and

(b) delivering it to a person on the premises or, if no person to whom it can be delivered is found there, fixing it to a conspicuous part of the premises.

Offences
16.- (1) If –

(a) an occupier of land or premises refuses to permit a person to do anything which he is entitled to do with regard to the land or premises under section 8(1) or (5); and

(b) the occupier knows or has reasonable cause to believe that the person is so entitled,

the occupier is guilty of an offence.

(2) If –

(a) a person hinders or obstructs a person in attempting to do anything which he is entitled to do with regard to land or premises under section 8 (1) or m(5); and

(b) the first-mentioned person knows or has reasonable cause to believe that the other person is so entitled,

the first-mentioned person is guilty of an offence.

(3) A person guilty of an offence under subsection (1) or (2) is liable on summary conviction to a fine of an amount not exceeding level 3 on the standard scale.

Recovery of sums.
17. – Any sum payable in pursuance of this Act (otherwise than by way of fine) shall be recoverable summarily as a civil debt.

Exception in case of Temples etc.
18.- (1) This Act shall not apply to land which is situated in inner London and in which there is an interest belonging to –

(a) the Honourable Society of the Inner Temple,

(b) the Honourable Society of the Middle Temple,

(c) the Honourable Society of Lincoln's Inn, or

(d) the Honourable Society of Gray's Inn.

(2) The reference in subsection (1) to inner London is to Greater London other than the outer London boroughs.

The Crown.
19. – (10 This Act shall apply to land in which there is –

(a) an interest belonging to Her Majesty in right of the Crown,

(b) an interest belonging to a government department, or

(c) an interest held in trust for Her Majesty for the purposes of any such department.

(2) This Act shall apply to –

(a) land which is vested in, but not occupied by, Her Majesty in right of the Duchy of Lancaster;

(b) land which is vested in, but not occupied by, the possessor for the time being of the Duchy of Cornwall.

Interpretation.
20.- In this Act, unless the context otherwise requires, the following expressions have the meanings hereby respectively assigned to them

"adjoining owner" and "adjoining occupier" respectively mean any owner and any occupier of land, buildings storeys or rooms adjoining those of the building owner and for the purposes only of section 6 within the distances specified in that section;

"appointing officer" means the person appointed under this Act by the local authority to make such appointments as are required under section 10(8);

"building owner" means an owner of land who is desirous of exercising rights under this Act;

"foundation", in relation to a wall, means the solid ground or artificially formed support resting on solid ground on which the wall rests;

"owner" includes –

(a) a person in receipt of, or entitled to receive, the whole or part of the rents or profits of land;

(b) a person in possession of land, otherwise than as a mortgagee or as a tenant from year to year or for a lesser term or as a tenant at will;

(c) a purchaser of an interest in land under contract for purchase or under an agreement for a lease, otherwise than under an agreement for a tenancy from year to year or for a lesser term;

"party fence wall" means a wall (not being part of a building) which stands on lands of different owners and is used or constructed to be used for separating such adjoining land of one owner the artificially formed support of which projects into the land of another owner;

"party structure" means a party wall and also a floor partition or other structure separating buildings or parts of buildings approached solely by means of separate staircases or separate entrances;

"party wall" means –

(a) a wall which forms part of a building and stands on lands of different owners to a greater extent than the projection of any artificially formed support on which the wall rests: and

(b) so much of a wall not being a wall referred to in paragraph (a) above as separates buildings belonging to different owners;

"special foundations" means foundations in which an assemblage of beams and rods is employed for the purpose of distributing any load; and

"surveyor" means any person not being a party to the matter appointed or selected under section 10 to determine disputes in accordance with the procedures set out in this Act.

Other statutory provisions.

22. – (1) The Secretary of State may by order amend or repeal any provision of a private or local Act passed before or in the same session as this Act, if it appears to him necessary or expedient to do so in consequence of this Act.

(2) An order under subsection (1) may –

(a) contain such savings or transitional provisions as the Secretary of State thinks fit;

(b) make different provision for different purposes.

(3) The power to make an order under subsection (1) shall be exercisable by statutory instrument subject to annulment in pursuance of a resolution of either House of Parliament.

General

22. – (1) This Act may be cited as the Party Wall etc. Act 1996.

(2) This Act shall come into force in accordance with provision made by the Secretary of State by order made by statutory instrument.

(3) An order under subsection (2) may –

> (a) contain such savings or transitional provisions as the Secretary of State thinks fit;

> (b) make different provision for different purposes.

(4) This Act extends to England and Wales only.

Part IX
Further Information

If you are not sure whether the Act applies to the work that you are planning, you should seek professional advice.

The Faculty of Party Wall Surveyors is an educational body concerned with party wall matters. It is non-profit making and is dedicated to providing the public with an understanding of the Act.

The Faculty runs an advice line and has a list of members in all areas to assist you in party wall matters. It can usually provide you with a party wall surveyor in your area.

The Faculty of Party Wall Surveyors (FPWS)
P O Box 86
Rye
TN31 9BN

Telephone: 01424 883300
Email: enq@fpws.org.uk
Website: www.fpws.org.uk

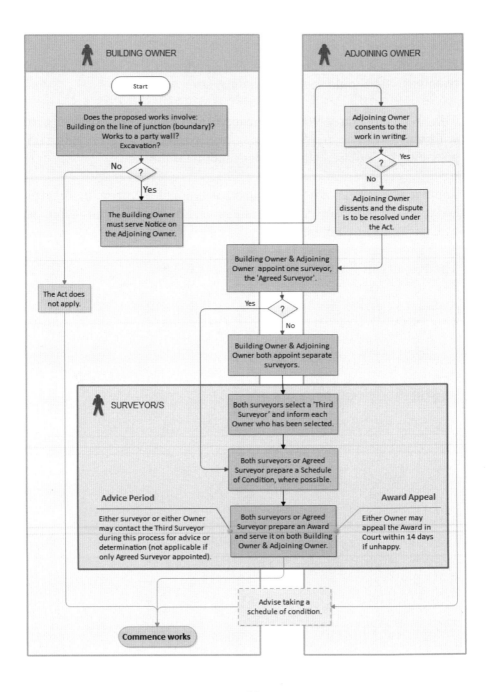

BUILDING OWNER

ADJOINING OWNER

Start

Does the proposed works involve:
Building on the line of junction (boundary)?
Works to a party wall?
Excavation?

Adjoining Owner
consents to the
work in writing.

No ?

Yes

Yes

No

The Building Owner
must serve Notice on
the Adjoining Owner.

Adjoining Owner
dissents and the dispute
is to be resolved under
the Act.

The Act does
not apply.

Building Owner & Adjoining
Owner appoint one surveyor,
the 'Agreed Surveyor'.

Yes ?

No

Building Owner & Adjoining
Owner both appoint separate
surveyors.

SURVEYOR/S

Both surveyors select a 'Third
Surveyor' and inform each
Owner who has been selected.

Both surveyors or Agreed
Surveyor prepare a Schedule
of Condition, where possible.

Advice Period

Either surveyor or either Owner
may contact the Third Surveyor
during this process for advice or
determination (not applicable if
only Agreed Surveyor appointed).

Both surveyors or Agreed
Surveyor prepare an Award
and serve it on both Building
Owner & Adjoining Owner.

Award Appeal

Either Owner may
appeal the Award in
Court within 14 days
if unhappy.

Advise taking a
schedule of condition.

Commence works

80

The Act and related Statutory Instruments

Party Wall etc. Act 1996
published by HMSO, ISBN 0-10-544096-5

Party Wall etc. Act 1996 (Commencement) Order 1997 (SI 1997/670 (c.24))
published by TSO, ISBN 011-064-2139

Party Wall etc. Act 1996 (Repeal of Local Enactments) Order 1997 (SI 1997/671)
published by TSO, ISBN 011-064-2120

Other publications

Party Wall etc. Act 1996
Misunderstandings and Guidance (second edition)
Published by The Faculty of Party Wall Surveyors
ISBN 9780955099564

Party Wall etc. Act 1996
The Third Surveyor – A Guide
Published by The Faculty of Party Wall Surveyors
ISBN 9780955099557

Party Wall etc. Act 1996
CPD Study Course
Published by The Faculty of Party Wall Surveyors
ISBN 9780955099588